Story by Maria Bird

Illustrated by Matvyn Wright

BROCKHAMPTON PRESS

Andy Pandy has a very special kind of Teddy Bear. He can walk and talk and is quite the nicest friend any little boy could have. He is not as big as Andy Pandy, but he tries to do everything Andy does.

One day Teddy said, 'I wish I could see a REAL BEAR.' 'We will go to the Zoo, and then you can see one,' said Andy Pandy. 'Will it be as big as me?' Teddy asked. Andy laughed. 'Much, much bigger,' he said.

When they got to the Zoo they saw big lions and striped tigers and funny monkeys and kangaroos. One of the kangaroos had a baby in a little pocket in front. 'If I had a pocket,' said Teddy, 'I'd put a hanky in it, not a baby kangaroo.'

ZOO

When they came to the REAL BEARS, Teddy could hardly believe his eyes. Even the little bears rolling over and over were much bigger than Teddy, and the mother bear was much, much, much, much, much, much bigger.

The young bears looked very helpless, but they were VERY BIG. Teddy stayed close to Andy Pandy.

'Don't you want to be a real bear?' asked Andy.

'No,' said Teddy, 'I would rather be your little bear.'

'I like bears very much,' said Teddy, 'but I want to see some other animals now, please.' So they left the bears, and soon found themselves in front of a fence, and behind the fence was an even bigger animal with a very long neck. It was a giraffe.

Andy Pandy and Teddy looked up and there at the end of the long neck was a kind face that looked as if it were smiling. 'What a nice animal,' said Andy. 'I do like it.' The giraffe brought her head down to have a look at them.

The giraffe had gentle brown eyes with long eyelashes. She had wide ears, and two little horns that looked as if they were covered with velvet. Andy helped Teddy up on to the fence so that he could see.

'I must stroke them,' said Teddy. He put his own furry paws on to the giraffe's horns, and suddenly the giraffe lifted up her long neck and there was Teddy, holding on to the horns, and sailing high up into the air.

He held on tight, and a long way down he could see Andy Pandy looking up. 'Come down,' Andy called. 'Pat her ears so that she knows to come down.' So Teddy patted the giraffe's ears, but his paws were so soft that the giraffe didn't feel them.

After a time the giraffe brought her long neck down again. And there was Andy Pandy ready to rescue Teddy. But no sooner had he taken hold of Teddy than up went the giraffe again, and there was Andy sailing up into the air as well.

Andy Pandy wriggled round to one of the gentle-looking ears, and put his face in it. Then he said, 'Please, giraffe, we have come up here by mistake, and should very much like to be taken down again.'

The giraffe twitched her ears to show that she understood, then she lowered her neck down and when her head had nearly touched the ground, she gave it a gentle shake, and off fell Andy Pandy and Teddy on to the soft grass.

The giraffe was most surprised when she saw the two strange little people who had fallen off. She thought they looked very nice, and she smiled at them and put her head down so that they could stroke her horns.

When they got home they couldn't stop talking about the wonderful day they had had at the Zoo. Teddy wished that the bears hadn't been quite so big, but he and Andy thought the giraffe was the very nicest animal they had ever seen.

a selection from the full list of

ANDY PANDY BOOKS

1 Andy Pandy and the willow tree
2 Andy Pandy and the white kitten
3 Andy Pandy and Teddy at the zoo

5 Andy Pandy's tea party
6 Andy Pandy and the gingerbread man
7 Andy Pandy in the country
8 Andy Pandy's shop
9 Andy Pandy's jack-in-the-box
11 Andy Pandy paints his house
12 Andy Pandy and the hedgehog
13 Andy Pandy's washing day

14 Andy Pandy and his hobby horse
15 Andy Pandy's kite
16 Andy Pandy's puppy
17 Andy Pandy and the teddy dog
18 Andy Pandy's dovecot
22 Andy Pandy and the snowman
24 Andy Pandy's new pet

25 Andy Pandy plays lions and tigers
26 Andy Pandy's playhouse
29 Andy Pandy and the scarecrow
30 Andy Pandy's red motor car
31 Andy Pandy and the yellow dog
32 Andy Pandy and the spotted cow

Printed in Great Britain for Brockhampton Press Ltd., Salisbury Road, Leicester
by Purnell & Sons Ltd., Paulton, Bristol.

11 12 13 14 15